The Legend of Bearby the Knight: A Sports Fable
© 1993
ISBN 0930899121

Written by Terry Whittaker
Illustrations by Myla Smith

Published By: Fanatic Publishing
                P.O. Box 586
                Columbus, Indiana 47202
                812-378-9677

Produced in Indiana
        Color Separations-
                Rheitone, Inc. Indianapolis
        Printing-
                The Benham Press, Indianapolis

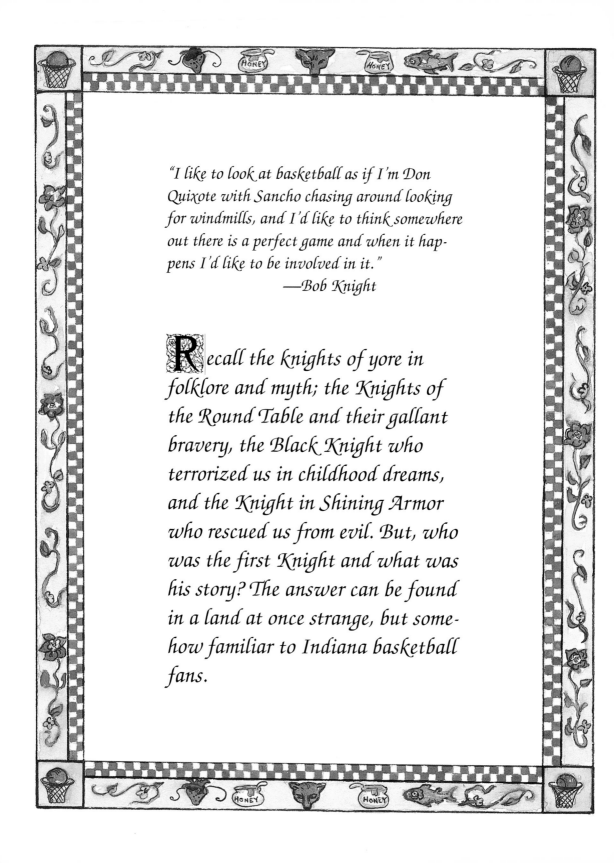

"I like to look at basketball as if I'm Don Quixote with Sancho chasing around looking for windmills, and I'd like to think somewhere out there is a perfect game and when it happens I'd like to be involved in it."
—Bob Knight

Recall the knights of yore in folklore and myth; the Knights of the Round Table and their gallant bravery, the Black Knight who terrorized us in childhood dreams, and the Knight in Shining Armor who rescued us from evil. But, who was the first Knight and what was his story? The answer can be found in a land at once strange, but somehow familiar to Indiana basketball fans.

Once upon a time, a young bear named Bearby Knight was summoned by the King of the Hoosbears to the Great Hall.

As he entered the Hall, Bearby once again wondered who had designed this abomination. For more bears wished to see games than the Hall would hold, and although seats went far up on both sides there were few on the ends.

Bearby approached the King, giving only a token bow as he was not a bear to kowtow even to his ruler. "Bearby," the King spoke, "it is with sadness that I look around my Hall and see that no banners of victory have been hung here for almost two decades." Bearby knew that not since the Hoosbears had been led by the one known simply as "The Bear" had victory been theirs. "I have chosen you to lead my charges," said the King. "Gather a small band of courageous soldiers, and return to me with the Banner of Champions."

"Sire, I shall do your bidding, but there are not enough brave warriors in our kingdom to vanquish all foes, so I must venture into the land of the Illini and return with the Mighty Quinn and into the land of the Buckeyes and find May the Scott. With them, I may then coerce the Benson of Kent from the nearby new castle and Wilker's cub (who was also named Bearby) from the Heights of Madison to join our band."

"Go forth," commanded the King, "and may the Great Bear be with you."

Bearby went first to his former teacher, Fred the Tailor, who, besides sewing the finest uniforms in the land, had won the Banner of Champions for the King of the Buckeyes with a group of cubs that included the young Bearby. "Be true to your cause and you shall prevail," said the Tailor, "but remember you have only four years to work with each warrior to prepare him for battle, unless they leave earlier to play for the NBA, the National Bears Association."

Bearby worked diligently with his troops, and although they won most battles, in the end they were always vanquished. Eventually his work truly bore honey. His band of warriors defeated all foes until but a handful stood in the way of the elusive Banner of Champions. But, alas, May the Scott's paw was broken in a fierce contest with the archrivals from Beardue. Later, without the Scott, enemies from the land of the Wildcats defeated the Hoosbears. Bearby vowed that his last year with this group would lead to ultimate victory.

The next year, as his charges defeated every foe, Bearby's anxiety grew, and he incurred the wrath of many Hoosbear fans when he angrily yanked the fur of young Wisbear during a heated contest.

Still, with the Scott leading them into the final battle with his bagpipe, Bearby's crew finally brought home the banner to the Great Hall.

"Well done," the King exclaimed, "but your work is not finished, for I now desire even more banners for my Hall. I have been told by my fortuneteller that a young bear from the land of the Illini, Sir Isiah of St. Joseph's, may lead us in victory. But first you must go into that land and bring him to us. You must beware however of the dreaded LouDoosa, a creature whose fur is arranged in such a ridiculous way on the top of his head, that any bear looking directly at him will die of uncontrollable laughter."

Bearby ventured into the foreign land and not far in his journey he came up behind a peculiar-looking bruin. Against his will Bearby's eyes began to wander along the bear's swooping fur which began near his ear and traveled in a tortured route completely around his skull. As the bear turned to face him, Bearby raised his highly polished shield. Looking at his own reflection, the LouDoosa exploded in a loud shriek of laughter, and continued giggling madly to himself as Bearby left.

As prophesied, Sir Isiah did eventually lead the Hoosbears to another banner, but even with his success many were not happy with Bearby.

In bear language there are 20 different words for fur, and Bearby could use each one in a most degrading manner when motivating his young charges in battle. And those scribes who approached him at the wrong time were often subjected to humiliation.

Many questioned Bearby's use of the witches' cauldron for cerebral reversal. When one of his charges was doing poorly in battle, Bearby would require him to sit in the cauldron until his behavior changed. Much to the displeasure of his critics, this often worked.

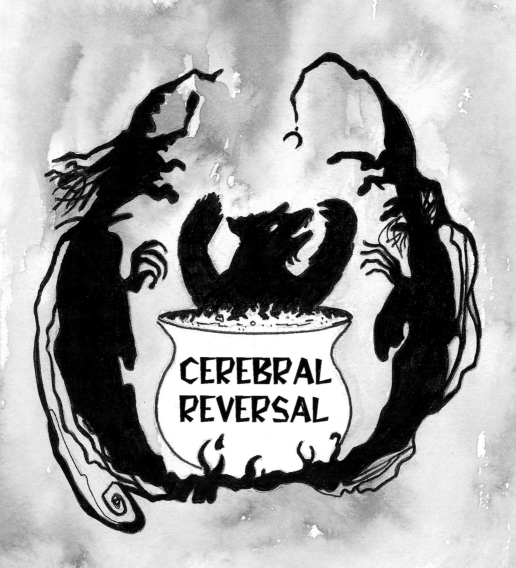

*O*ne year, frustrated at the play of his team, Bearby cancelled the annual bears' picnic. Oh, the uproar was great, as fans of the Hoosbears bemoaned the loss of the feast, for they were no longer to see their heroes gorge themselves on fish and rub against trees. But, as with most of the controversies surrounding Bearby, this was soon forgotten.

Bearby also got into great feuds with the leaders of opposing armies including Friedbear of the Wolverines, Brown Bear of the Tigers, and of course LouDoosa of the Illini.

*B*ut, Bearby's worst transgression occurred during a particularly frustrating season. Angered once too often by the striped bears who saw that the rules of battle were followed, Bearby grabbed the King's throne* (happily without the King on it, as he was not in attendance), and hurled it onto the floor of the Hall.

*The word, throne, actually came into the language because of this incident. Originally known only as the King's chair, it became the "King's thrown chair." Later the word chair was dropped and the spelling of thrown altered.

*L*ater, Bearby apologized to the King, but told him that he was not happy. "Sire, I fear we may never win again. Even though I ventured to the new castle for Allfur as you requested, and brought back Uwe the Giant from across the great sea, we are poor in battle. The Giant has bad paws and often drops his weapon, and Allfur, although fierce when we charge, appears to be hibernating when we are on the defensive."

"Fear not," spoke the King, "for it has been foretold that Allfur shall bring us ultimate victory."

Eventually, even with the high expectations, as predicted, young Allfur did lead the Hoosbears to victory over the men of orange and Bearby returned with yet another banner for the Hall.

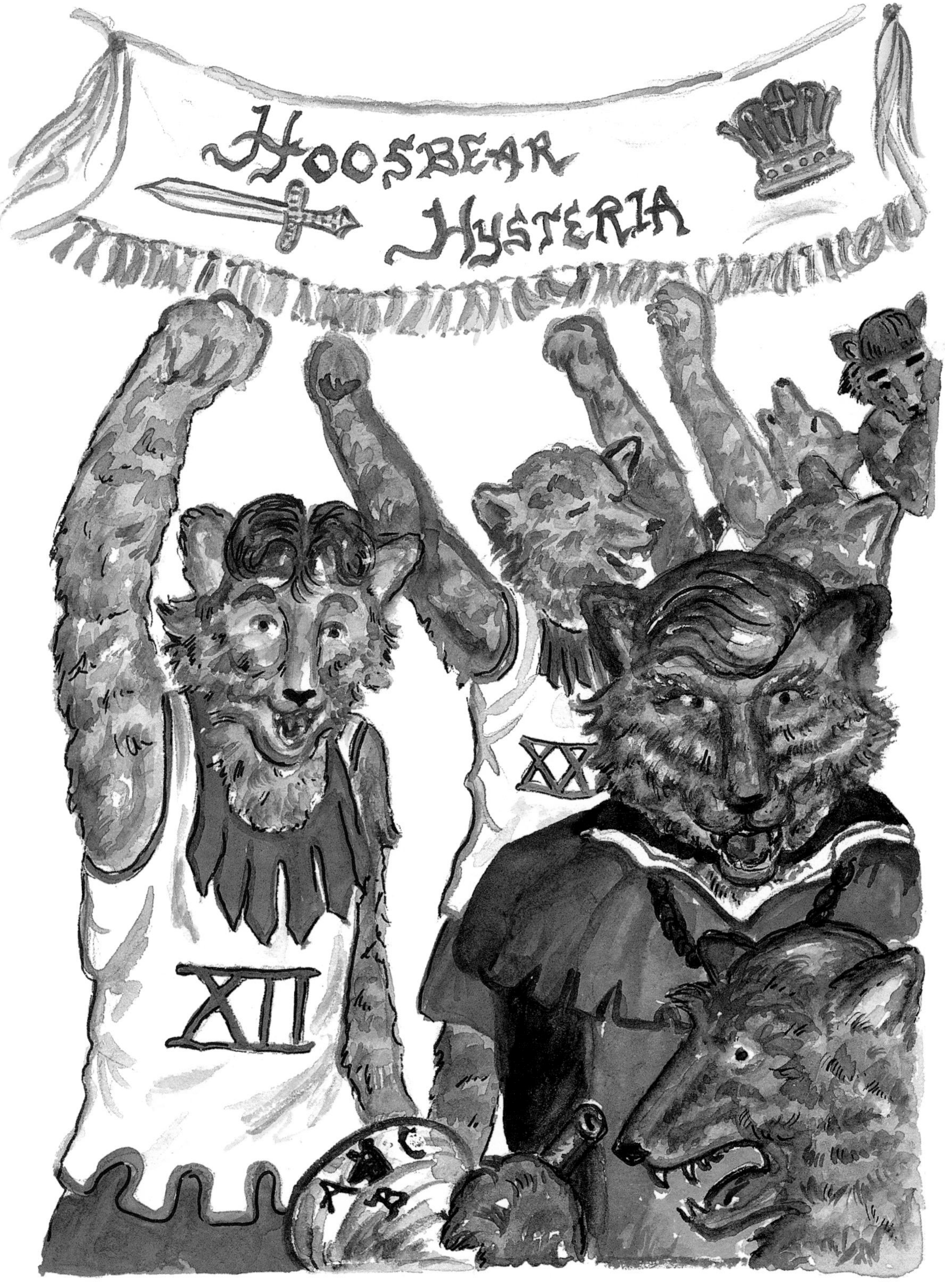
HOOSBEAR
HYSTERIA
XX
XII

The Great Hall was an exciting place to be during these times, and perhaps no bear better represented the hysteria than a commentator for the American Bearcasting Corporation. Although he amused many, his continuous rapid descriptions annoyed many others. "Hey baby," he might say, "this bear's a candidate for my all-Goldilocks team . . . looks great until there's a little pressure on, and then he runs away." Or, "This team is all finished, might as well take them to the den, tell them it's Winter and leave a wake-up call for Spring."

All the kingdom praised Bearby, but he was not happy. "My King, I have done all that you have asked and brought great honor to your kingdom, but I have grown weary of the battle."

"Things are not as they once were when young cubs played for the love of the game. Alas, I fear that many of our foes give young bears riches to fight for them. When we travel to do battle at other arenas, we often see the steeds of our opponents tethered outside, beautiful mustangs and broncos which they surely could not afford. We also hear that many live in luxurious dens and are given great hordes of honey."

"*I* also fear that our youth have become lazy," continued Bearby. "On a recent journey I spied some young cubs tossing an old wasp's nest through a basket nailed high on a tree. I shouted at them, 'Get thee to thy den and practice the art of battle,' but they only laughed. I said, 'Do you not know who I am?' and they replied, 'Yes, a silly old bear in battered armor.' Alas, my sire, I fear they may be right."

"Bearby," responded the King, "you have truly done great service to the realm. I ask only one last thing of you. Travel to the bailey just to the south. There we have heard reports of a marvelous young bear named Sir Damon. I must have your opinion of his worth."

Within a few days Bearby returned to the Great Hall. "Sire," Bearby spoke with a gleam in his eye, "Sir Damon is all that you have heard. He is better than any we have now. If he could be teamed with our young Calbear, we might even be able to compete with great foes like the devils of blue."

As valiantly as Calbear and Sir Damon fought, they fell just short of winning another banner. After the bitter defeat, Bearby requested an audience with the King. "Sire, with Sir Damon and the others returning we will have brave warriors to do battle next year. However, we will need someone strong to defend our center. Fortunately, I know of just such a bear."

"And who might that be?" asked the King.

"His name is Ivan Bearenko, * and he lives far away over the great sea," explained Bearby. "Some doubt he exists, but I assure you he is very real. He lives in the heart of every cub who longs to fight for our Hoosbears, and in the dreams of every one of our loyal followers. It shall be my quest to find him and bring him back to the Great Hall. I will venture forth alone for this is a dangerous journey."

"*W*ill you not even take your trusted servant, Brad Bombear?"

"No, sire, there are some things a bear must do by himself."

"May the stars of Ursa guide you."

"Thank you, sire, I will do my best, but as you know, sometimes you get the bear and sometimes the bear gets you."

With a farewell to the King, Bearby mounted his steed and rode off toward the setting sun.

*You can help Bearby search for Ivan. He is somewhere in several of the pictures in this book. He looks like this:

*E*pilogue:

After Bearby's illustrious career the honorary title of Knight was given only to the most brave and successful warriors. Bearby became so successful that he later graduated in rank from Knight to General.